Preface by Ti

The Enduring P

Few works in martial literature oɪɪeɪ uie ɪaw ___ ,   l unfiltered wisdom found in *The Book of Five Rings*. Composed in 1645 by Miyamoto Musashi—a swordsman undefeated in over sixty duels—this text is not just about fighting. It is a guide to mastering conflict, perception, and the self.

Unlike many classical texts, *The Book of Five Rings* wasn't designed for public acclaim or formal instruction. Musashi wrote it in seclusion near the end of his life, intending it as a personal transmission of strategic truth. His goal wasn't to impress with flowery theory, but to teach what works. What you find here is stripped of ornament—blunt, practical, and deeply philosophical.

The structure of the book reflects the elements: Ground, Water, Fire, Wind, and Void. Each represents a different layer of strategy, from posture and presence to adaptability, criticism of other schools, and the final dissolution of form into instinct. Through these five scrolls, Musashi speaks to warriors—not only those of the sword, but those facing any form of challenge.

This edition draws from multiple sources and traditions, many of which are fragmentary, retranslated, or adapted from earlier versions. It is not a direct translation from one Japanese manuscript but an interpretive reconstruction guided by clarity and intent. Where necessary, annotations have been added to clarify cultural references, technical language, or philosophical nuance.

What matters most is that these teachings are still relevant. Musashi's words speak to artists, athletes, entrepreneurs, leaders—anyone who walks a path that demands discipline, timing, and the ability to act without hesitation.

To study this book is not just to read about strategy—it is to live it.

Who Was Miyamoto Musashi?

Miyamoto Musashi (c. 1584–1645) is widely regarded as Japan's greatest swordsman. A master duelist, strategist, and artist, he won more than sixty sword fights—many to the death—and never lost. He developed the Ni-Tō Ichi-ryū ("Two Swords, One School") style, emphasizing adaptability, precision, and the use of both long and short swords together.

Unlike many warriors of his time, Musashi valued no single weapon or technique above insight. He believed true mastery came not from form or tradition, but from understanding timing, rhythm, and the heart of conflict itself. Toward the end of his life,

The Book of Five Rings

by Miyamoto Musashi

Complete Edition

The New Modern English Translation
(Translated and Annotated)

Author – Miyamoto Musashi

Editor – Timeless Lore

Translator – Nathan Cole

TABLE OF CONTENTS

he withdrew to a cave in Kyushu and wrote *The Book of Five Rings*—a final summation of his life's path, intended for serious students of strategy.

About This Edition

This edition of *The Book of Five Rings* presents a modern, accessible interpretation of the strategic philosophy of Miyamoto Musashi. Rather than relying on a single source text, it draws on a comparative reading of multiple surviving manuscripts—most of which are handwritten copies dating from the Edo period and passed down through Musashi's students and later scholars.

No known original manuscript by Musashi's own hand has survived, and scholars believe that the original document— reportedly dictated to or handed over to his disciple Teruo Magonojo—was lost or copied shortly after its creation in 1645. Today, there are several extant versions of the text in Japanese archives and private collections, each with small variations in language or order.

As such, *The Book of Five Rings* exists in the public domain, and all modern editions, including this one, are based on reconstructed texts that reflect the spirit and structure of the original without claiming to reproduce a definitive or canonical version.

This volume offers not a literal translation but a contemporary retelling with annotations, commentary, and structured interpretation, designed to help modern readers understand and apply Musashi's ideas across disciplines—from leadership to personal growth, business strategy to martial arts.

Introduction

I've spent many years deeply immersed in the Way of strategy, known as Ni Ten Ichi Ryu—the School of the Two Heavens as One. Now, for the first time, I have decided to write down what I have learned. It is the beginning of the tenth month in the twentieth year of the Kanei era, the year 1645. I've ascended Mount Iwato in Higo Province, on the island of Kyushu, to offer my respects to the heavens, pray to the Goddess Kwannon, and bow before the Buddha.

I am a warrior from Harima Province. My full name is Shinmen Musashi-no-Kami Fujiwara no Geshin, and I am now sixty years old.

From a young age, I've been drawn to the Way of strategy. I fought my first duel at the age of thirteen, defeating a martial artist from the Shinto school named Arima Kihei. At sixteen, I bested another skilled fighter, Tadashima Akiyama. By twenty-one, I had traveled to the capital, where I faced many different strategists, winning every match I fought.

After that, I continued to travel across the provinces, challenging and defeating practitioners from various schools of martial strategy. I never lost a single contest, even after engaging in over sixty duels between the ages of thirteen and about twenty-eight or twenty-nine.

When I turned thirty, I began to reflect on those past victories. I realized they weren't due to a complete understanding of strategy. Maybe I succeeded because of natural talent, or perhaps it was fate, or simply that my opponents' methods were lacking. After that, I dedicated myself to studying strategy relentlessly, morning and night. Eventually, around the age of fifty, I came to fully understand the true Way of strategy.

Since then, I've lived without adhering to any specific school or doctrine. With the insight gained through strategy, I've practiced and developed many skills on my own—without a teacher or guide.

In writing this book, I haven't drawn on the teachings of Buddhism or Confucianism, nor have I relied on old war stories or manuals on military tactics. Instead, I take up my brush to reveal the true essence of this Ichi school, as it reflects the spirit of the heavens and the presence of Kwannon.

It is now the night of the tenth day of the tenth month, and the time is the Hour of the Tiger—between three and five in the morning.

The Ground Book

Strategy is the discipline of the warrior[1]. It's something that commanders must put into practice, and something every soldier should understand. Yet in today's world, there are no warriors who truly grasp the real path of strategy.

There are many different "Ways" in life. There's **the Way of Salvation through Buddhism, the scholarly Way of Confucius**[2], the medical Way of the doctor, **the poetic Way of Waka**[3], and also the arts like tea ceremony, archery, and countless others. Each person follows the Way that suits them best.

It's often said that the warrior's path is a combination of both **pen and sword—meaning learning and combat.**[4] A warrior

---

[1] **"Strategy is the discipline of the warrior."** - Musashi uses "strategy" (兵法, hyōhō) not just to mean tactics, but a complete way of life, encompassing combat, mindset, and leadership.

[2] **"The Way of Salvation through Buddhism, the scholarly Way of Confucius…"** - This reflects the influence of Chinese philosophy on Japanese thought during the Edo period; Buddhism and Confucianism were two dominant cultural forces.

[3] **"The poetic Way of Waka…"** - Waka is a classical Japanese poetic form, often used by aristocrats to express refined emotion or courtly love, considered one of the high arts.

[4] **"Pen and sword—meaning learning and combat."** - A famous Japanese phrase (文武両道, bunbu ryōdō), promoting the ideal balance between scholarly learning and martial ability.

should appreciate both of these. Even without natural talent, someone can still become a warrior by committing themselves fully to both parts of this path.

At its core, the Way of the warrior means accepting death without hesitation. Now, others too—monks, women, peasants, even those of the lowest ranks—may sacrifice their lives out of duty or shame, but that's not the same thing. What makes the warrior different is that his study of strategy is aimed at overcoming others. Whether by winning one-on-one duels or leading armies into battle, victory brings honor and influence to the warrior and to the lord he serves. This is the true power of strategy.

The Way of Strategy

In both China and Japan, those who devoted themselves to this art were known as masters of strategy. All warriors must study this Way.

These days, there are people who rise in society calling themselves strategists, but most are simply sword fighters. The followers of the **Kashima and Katori shrines in Hitachi province**[5] claimed to receive their knowledge from the gods, and based their schools

---

[5] **"Kashima and Katori shrines in Hitachi province…"** - Refers to the **Kashima Shintō-ryū** and **Katori Shintō-ryū**, two of Japan's oldest martial arts schools, both associated with divine inspiration and ritualized swordsmanship.

on that wisdom, traveling the land to teach others. This is what people now think of as strategy.

But in the old days, strategy was counted among the **Ten Skills and the Seven Arts**[6]—a discipline that brought real benefit. Yes, it was a martial art, but its value went far beyond sword fighting. The true purpose of swordsmanship can't be fully understood just by mastering technique.

Today, if you look around, you'll see that many arts have become commodities. People use their tools and knowledge as a way to sell themselves. It's like a flower and its seed—the flower is admired, while the seed that gives life to it is ignored. This kind of flashy "strategy" is about appearance more than substance. Both the teachers and the students focus on style, showing off their moves and techniques, rushing to make the flower bloom too soon. They boast about "this dojo" or "that dojo" and treat the art as a business. Someone once said, **"Immature strategy leads to suffering."**[7] That was wise.

---

[6] **"Ten Skills and the Seven Arts"** - This refers to classical Chinese and Japanese ideas of elite education—covering military and civil arts expected of a well-rounded noble.

[7] **"Immature strategy leads to suffering."** - Possibly a paraphrase of a traditional Japanese proverb or a personal maxim by Musashi—warns against superficial skill without depth.

There are four basic paths people follow in life: the path of the noble, the farmer, the craftsman, and the merchant.

First, the farmer. With his tools, he works the land through the changing seasons, always aware of nature's timing.

Second, the merchant. The sake brewer gathers ingredients and uses them to make his living. A merchant's way is to live through the pursuit of profit. That is his Way.

Third, the noble warrior. He carries weapons as part of his profession, and his Way is to understand and master their use. If a noble doesn't care for strategy, he'll fail to understand the value of those weapons. Shouldn't he at least appreciate it a little?

Fourth, the craftsman. The carpenter's Way is to master his tools—he begins by planning with accuracy, using precise measurements, and then follows through with skilled hands. This is how he moves through life.

These are the four main Ways: the Way of the noble, the farmer, the craftsman, and the merchant.

Comparing the Way of the Carpenter to Strategy

The path of a carpenter can be compared to the way of strategy through the idea of building homes. There are homes of the aristocracy, homes of warriors, **the Four Houses**[8], homes that fall into ruin, homes that flourish, family traditions, house styles, and household names. Just as a carpenter works from a blueprint, the strategist must plan their campaign. If you're serious about mastering the art of war, reflect carefully on what's written in this book. **The teacher is like a needle, guiding the thread**[9]— that's the student. Constant, focused practice is essential.

Just like a lead carpenter, a military commander must understand the natural order of things, the customs of the land, and the traditions of families. This is the essence of leadership.

The master carpenter must know how to design structures like towers and temples, be familiar with palace layouts, and guide teams to bring buildings to life. In the same way, a skilled commander oversees the building and management of a warrior household.

In house construction, wood is chosen carefully. Smooth, straight timber without knots is selected for the visible pillars. Slightly

---

[8] **"The Four Houses"** - Could refer to powerful samurai clans, or metaphorically to major schools of tradition—unclear without more context, but likely denotes societal structure.

[9] **"The teacher is like a needle, guiding the thread..."** - A traditional metaphor for mentorship in Japanese pedagogy—the teacher shapes and directs, the student must follow and internalize.

flawed wood, as long as it's mostly straight, can be used for inner supports. Wood that looks beautiful but isn't particularly strong can be used for doors, lintels, sliding panels, and thresholds. Even rugged, knotted wood has its place when used wisely in less visible parts. Timber that's too weak or too full of defects is best used for scaffolding or burned as firewood.

The lead carpenter assigns tasks based on each worker's strengths. Those with skill build the floors, door frames, and ceilings. Workers with less talent lay the floor beams or shape wedges and perform support tasks. If the foreman understands the capabilities of each person and puts them in the right roles, the final product will turn out well.

A good foreman is aware of both the skills and the limits of his crew. He checks in with them regularly, never making unreasonable demands. He should also be mindful of their morale, stepping in to motivate them when needed. This same principle applies to strategic leadership.

The Way of Strategy

Just like a soldier cares for his gear, a carpenter keeps his tools sharp. He carries them in a box and uses them under the guidance of his foreman. He uses an axe to shape beams and pillars, a plane to smooth shelves and floors, and carves intricate designs with precision, aiming to do the best work his abilities allow. This is the essence of craftsmanship.

Once a carpenter becomes skilled and understands measurements well, he can rise to the level of a foreman.

The true skill of the carpenter lies in creating fine items—**miniature shrines, writing desks, lanterns**[10], chopping boards, pot lids, and more. These are his specialties. This is also true for the trained warrior—you should reflect deeply on this comparison.

The mark of a master carpenter is that his work doesn't warp, his joints fit perfectly, and each piece connects seamlessly. It's not enough for the job to simply look finished—it must be aligned, smooth, and cohesive. This is crucial.

If you're serious about learning this Way, study each point in this book carefully and thoroughly. Only through deep investigation and dedicated practice will you truly understand.

Overview of the Five Books in This Strategy Manual

This book on strategy is divided into five separate scrolls, each

---

[10] **"Miniature shrines, writing desks, lanterns…"** - Examples of detailed, precise craftsmanship highly valued in Japanese culture, showing the subtle parallel between martial skill and fine artistry.

representing a distinct element: Earth, Water, Fire, Wind (meaning tradition), and **Void (emptiness).**[11]

The **Earth Book** lays the foundation for my strategic teachings as taught in my school, known as **Ichi-ryu**[12]. You can't truly understand strategy just by practicing swordsmanship. You must grasp both the minute and the massive, the shallow and the deep. Just like a road mapped out clearly on the ground, this first book establishes the groundwork of the path.

The **Water Book** comes next. Just like water, your spirit should be adaptable. Water changes to match the shape of whatever holds it — it can be calm or wild, gentle or forceful. Water is clear and pure, and through this clarity, the core teachings of the Ichi-ryu school are revealed. If you understand the key principles of combat, then defeating one opponent teaches you how to defeat any opponent. The mindset required to overcome a single man is the same mindset needed to defeat ten thousand. A skilled strategist knows how to expand simple things into complex forms — like constructing a giant Buddha from a tiny model. While I can't explain this fully in writing, the central idea is that by

---

[11] **"Void (emptiness)"** - In Zen Buddhism and Japanese philosophy, the Void (空, kū) represents formlessness, ultimate truth, and the transcendence of duality.

[12] **"Ichi-ryu" (一流)** - Literally "One School." Musashi's school emphasized flexibility, dual wielding, and philosophical depth beyond technique.

mastering one thing, you gain insight into many. The Water Book expands on this.

The **Fire Book** is focused on combat. Fire, whether it's small or large, burns with intensity — and battles are the same. Whether fighting one-on-one or in a massive army clash, the core spirit remains. It's important to recognize that things of great size are easy to notice and anticipate, while small things can be unpredictable. Armies are slow to shift, making their moves more obvious. Individuals, however, can change direction quickly, making their actions harder to foresee. This is a vital concept to understand. The key message of the Fire Book is the importance of consistent practice so you can act swiftly and decisively. Strategy must be integrated into everyday life, with unwavering focus. This book details the mindset needed for battle.

The **Wind Book** explores the methods of other schools. "Wind" here means the traditions — past and present — from various schools of swordsmanship. I break down their techniques clearly so you can understand what's commonly practiced elsewhere. Understanding others is the only way to truly understand yourself. Every path has distractions, and even a small deviation from the true Way can grow into a major one over time. What feels right in the moment may not align with the true path in the long run. Many schools have reduced strategy to nothing more than fencing techniques. That's not surprising — but my school teaches strategy as something deeper. Although we also use sword techniques, our core principle lies elsewhere. The Wind Book explains what typical strategy looks like in other traditions.

Finally, the **Void Book**. "Void" refers to that which has no form, no beginning, and no end. To grasp this is to transcend understanding itself. Strategy should reflect the natural order of the world. When you truly understand the flow of nature and can sense the rhythm of a situation, you'll be able to strike without effort or hesitation. This is the Way of the Void. In this book, I aim to show how to follow the true path in harmony with nature.

The Name "Ichi-ryu Ni-To" (One School – Two Swords)

Warriors — whether generals or foot soldiers — wear two swords. In the past, these were called the long sword and the short sword. Today, they're known as the **katana and the wakizashi**[13]. Regardless of the reason, in our culture, it's traditional for a warrior to carry both. This is an essential part of the warrior's path.

---

[13] **"Katana and the wakizashi"** - The traditional daishō (大小) sword pair carried by samurai: the **katana** (long sword) for open combat, the **wakizashi** (short sword) for close quarters or ritual suicide (seppuku).

The term **Nito Ichi-ryu** refers to the strategic use of both swords together. Spears and halberds are weapons suited for outdoor combat, but in the Ichi school, you should train from the beginning to wield a long sword in one hand and a short sword in the other. This reflects the truth of battle — when your life is on the line, you must use everything you have. It's a mistake to die with a weapon still sheathed.

Holding a sword in both hands can limit your range of motion, especially in complex environments like on horseback, rough terrain, muddy fields, rocky ground, or in crowded areas. My approach emphasizes wielding the long sword with one hand. This doesn't apply to heavier weapons like spears or halberds, but when it comes to swords, one-handed use is more versatile. Using both hands on a long sword is not ideal, particularly if you need your other hand to hold a bow or spear.

That said, if you're in a situation where using one hand isn't enough to strike your opponent effectively, then it's fine to use both hands. Learning to use a long sword in one hand may seem difficult at first — but everything is hard when you're just starting out. Drawing a bow or handling a halberd is also challenging in the beginning, but with practice, your strength and skill grow. As you train with the long sword, you will naturally develop the power and flow of the Way, and it will become second nature.

As I'll explain in the Water Book, speed is not the key to using the long sword well. The long sword should move in wide, sweeping motions, while the short sword is better used for close, compact strikes. This is one of the first things you must understand.

According to the Ichi school, victory does not depend on the size of the weapon — you can win with a long one or a short one. The essence of our strategy is about mastering the art of winning, regardless of the weapon or its length.

In battles with multiple opponents or when attempting to capture someone alive, using two swords is far more effective than just one. These ideas are difficult to put into words. But remember this principle: from one thing, understand ten thousand. Once you've mastered the Way of strategy, there will be nothing you can't perceive. Dedicate yourself fully to the study.

The Meaning Behind the Word "Strategy"

Those who have mastered the art of the long sword are known as strategists. In other martial disciplines, the names are more specific those skilled with the bow are archers, with the spear are spearmen, with firearms are marksmen, and with the halberd are halberdiers. But we don't refer to masters of the long sword simply as "swordsmen" or **"companionswordsmen."**[14] That's because the sword is not just another weapon it is the foundation of strategy itself.

Weapons like bows, guns, spears, and halberds are part of a warrior's toolkit, and they all serve strategic purposes. But the long sword is different. To master it is to master not just combat, but also leadership and personal discipline. It's through the sword that one learns to command both oneself and others. A true strategist can defeat ten opponents alone. And just as one man can overcome ten, ten can overcome a hundred, a hundred can defeat a thousand, and a thousand can triumph over ten thousand. That is the essence of my strategy: one man, fully trained, can be equal to an army. This is the complete art of the warrior.

The Way of the warrior is not the same as following other traditional paths like Confucianism, Buddhism, the arts, or dance. Still, while these paths are not the core of the Way, someone who understands the Way deeply will recognize its principles in all things. Everyone should polish and refine their own path.

---

[14] **"Companionswordsmen"** - This appears to be Musashi's own dismissal of simplistic terminology—his emphasis is on the strategist, not just the swordsman.

The Role of Weapons in Strategy

Every weapon has its proper use, and timing and environment play a big role in that.

The companion sword, which is shorter, is especially effective in tight spaces or when you're grappling closely with your opponent. The long sword, on the other hand, can be used efficiently in nearly every kind of situation.

In open battle, the halberd is less effective than the spear. The spear gives you the advantage of taking the initiative, while the halberd leans more toward defense. Between two equally skilled fighters, the one with the spear has a slight edge. Both weapons have their roles, but neither works well in tight quarters, and neither is good for capturing someone alive. They're designed for battlefield use.

If you only train in techniques suited for indoor or confined spaces, your thinking will become limited, and you'll struggle in real-world combat.

The bow shines at the beginning of a battle, especially on open terrain like a moor, because archers can fire from behind the front line. But it's less useful during a siege or when the enemy is farther than forty yards away. That's one reason traditional schools of archery have become rare it no longer has the same relevance.

When you're inside a fortress, no weapon beats the gun. It's unmatched before the battle lines meet. But once combat becomes close and swords are drawn, firearms are useless.

One of the advantages of archery is that you can visually follow the arrow and adjust your aim. You can't do that with bullets. Understanding this is important.

Just as a horse must be strong, healthy, and without defects, so must your weapons be reliable. Horses should walk with power, and swords both long and short should cut cleanly. Spears and halberds must be able to endure repeated strikes, and bows and guns must be durable and sturdy. What matters most is that your weapons are practical and tough, not flashy or ornamental.

Avoid favoring one weapon too much. Becoming overly attached to a single tool is just as harmful as not knowing it well enough. Don't blindly imitate others use what suits you best. A commander or soldier with strong preferences will be limited. You need to study all weapons seriously and thoroughly.

Timing in Strategy

Timing is everything. To master timing in strategy, you must practice it extensively.

This applies not just to combat, but to the arts as well dancing, playing instruments, and more all require good rhythm. The same is true for martial skills like archery, gunmanship, and horseback riding. Every discipline involves timing.

Even the Void the concept of nothingness has its own timing.

Throughout a warrior's life, there are cycles: growth and decline, harmony and conflict. The same goes for business the rise and fall of profit follows a rhythm. Everything moves according to timing, and it's your job to recognize that.

In strategy, many types of timing exist. From the very beginning, you need to understand which moments are right and which are wrong. Among big and small opportunities, fast and slow actions, you must identify the correct timing. First, recognize the timing based on distance and surroundings. That is the core of strategic thinking. Most of all, if you fail to grasp the "background timing," your entire strategy will be uncertain and weak.

Victory comes from using unexpected timing, born from understanding both the Void and your opponent's rhythm. If you can predict the enemy's timing and act in a way they don't foresee, you'll gain the upper hand.

All five sections of this book focus heavily on timing. You must train constantly to fully understand it.

By practicing the Ichi style of strategy day and night, your awareness will expand. My method applies both to large-scale warfare and personal, one-on-one combat. This is the first time I've written it all down in the five books: Ground, Water, Fire, Wind (Tradition), and Void.

If you want to truly learn my strategy, start here:

- Be honest in thought and action.

- Understand that mastery comes from constant practice.

- Learn about all forms of art and technique.

- Study every trade and profession.

- Know how to weigh gain and loss in worldly affairs.

- Develop intuitive judgment and insight into everything.

- Train yourself to notice what isn't visible.

- Pay attention to the smallest details.

- Don't waste time on useless actions.

Let these ideas guide your heart, and dedicate yourself to the Way of strategy. If you don't train your mind to see the big picture, you'll never master the path. But if you fully absorb these teachings, you'll be able to overcome twenty or thirty opponents without fail.

More importantly, if you commit yourself sincerely to this path, you'll begin to win fights not just with your body, but with your mind and spirit. You'll be able to control your own body effortlessly, defeat enemies with presence alone, and through serious training overcome ten men with just your spirit.

When you reach that level, won't that make you truly unbeatable?

In larger-scale strategy, a wise leader will know how to manage many people skillfully, act with integrity, govern wisely, and care for his people thus strengthening the state. If there is any path that embodies the spirit of never being defeated, that brings personal success and honor, it is the Way of strategy.

Written on the twelfth day of the fifth month, in the second year of **Shoho**[15] (1645).

Teruo Magonojo – SHINMEN MUSASHI

---

[15] The **Shohō era** was a short period during the rule of Tokugawa Iemitsu. Musashi wrote this book near the end of his life, while living in relative seclusion.

Analysis of The Ground Book

The Ground Book is Musashi's foundation for all strategy. It doesn't dive into techniques yet — instead, it explains what **strategy really is** and why it matters. For Musashi, strategy isn't just sword fighting; it's a **way of life**, combining discipline, combat, leadership, and clear perception.

He contrasts true warriors with those who only know swordplay. The real strategist must think beyond appearances — rejecting flashiness and focusing on **substance**. Using comparisons to farming, craftsmanship, and commerce, Musashi explains that every role in society has a "Way" — but the warrior's Way must involve both mastery of weapons and **mental clarity**.

He uses the image of the **carpenter** to illustrate leadership and precision. Just as a builder selects the right wood and tools for the job, a commander must know how to lead people and apply strategy with care. The strategist must constantly train body, mind, and perception to grasp timing, terrain, and the true purpose of each action.

Musashi also previews the rest of the book — explaining that it will be divided into five scrolls, each tied to an element: Earth, Water, Fire, Wind (meaning other schools), and Void. The **Earth Book** is the map — showing where the path begins.

Key Lessons from The Ground Book

1. **Strategy is more than combat** — it's a full path of discipline, awareness, and leadership.

2. **Form without purpose is empty** — true warriors value substance over show.

3. **Study every profession** — learning from farmers, merchants, and craftsmen sharpens your mind.

4. **Mastery comes from continuous, mindful practice.**

5. **Leadership is strategic craftsmanship** — like a carpenter choosing wood, a warrior must know his people and tools.

6. **Understand the big and the small** — from duels to armies, the principles are the same.

In short

The Ground Book sets the stage. Musashi teaches that strategy starts with **clear thinking**, **real discipline**, and **lifelong learning**. Before you even draw a sword, you need to understand yourself, your tools, and your place in the world. Strategy, he says, is about building something — not just destroying.

The Water Book

The mindset behind the **Ni Ten Ichi school of strategy**[16] is grounded in the nature of water—fluid, adaptable, and powerful. This section, called the Water Book, teaches how to achieve victory through the long sword technique, the signature form of this school. Words alone can't fully express the depth of the Way, but you can grasp it through experience and intuition. Read each line carefully, reflect on it, and let the meaning sink in deeply. If you take the teachings lightly or interpret them loosely, you'll lose sight of the true path.

The principles here are explained through the lens of one-on-one combat, but you should always think on a larger scale—imagine armies of ten thousand. Strategy is unlike any other discipline: a small misstep can lead you astray and into confusion or poor habits.

Reading this book once is not enough to understand the Way of strategy. You must absorb its teachings—not just read, memorize, or mimic. You need to internalize the lessons, studying until they become second nature, both in mind and body.

---

[16] **"Ni Ten Ichi school of strategy"** - The school founded by Musashi, meaning "Two Heavens, One School," famous for using both the long and short swords together.

The Spirit in Strategy

Your mindset in battle should not differ from your everyday state of mind. Whether you're fighting or simply living, be firm yet composed. Face all situations with confidence—not tension, not recklessness. Let your spirit be calm but unshaken, alert but not biased.

Even when you feel inner stillness, your body must not go limp. And when your body is at ease, keep your spirit sharp. Do not let your physical state disturb your mind, nor your thoughts affect your posture. Avoid being too passive or overly intense. Both extremes are weak. A heightened spirit lacks stability, and a dull spirit lacks power.

Keep your inner state hidden from your opponent. If you're small in stature, learn how those larger than you think and move. If you're large, understand the rhythm of those who are smaller. Never rely solely on your own body's reactions—stay aware and keep your perspective broad and unobstructed.

To grow in strategy, you must also sharpen your wisdom. Learn justice, understand right from wrong, and study various disciplines one by one. When you can no longer be deceived or shaken by others, you'll know you're beginning to grasp the strategic mindset.

This kind of wisdom is unlike any other. Even under pressure in battle, you must continue studying the principles so your mind stays steady and your strategy strong.

Posture in Strategy

Keep your head upright—not slouched, tilted, or twisted. Your forehead and the space between your eyes should remain smooth. Avoid excessive blinking or darting your eyes around. Narrow your eyes slightly and maintain a composed expression.

Align your nose in a straight line and feel a slight flare in your nostrils. Hold the back of your neck straight and let your energy extend from the top of your head down through your entire body. Relax your shoulders and strengthen your legs all the way from your knees to your toes. Brace your core to avoid bending at the waist. Secure your short sword tightly against your abdomen with your belt—this is called **"wedging in."**[17]

In strategy, your battle posture and your daily posture should become one and the same. Practice this until it becomes natural.

Vision in Strategy

Train your eyes to take in the full scene—wide and expansive.

---

[17] **"Wedging in" the short sword** - A practical way of securing the short sword (wakizashi) tightly at the waist—standard for samurai in preparation for movement.

This is called the **"twofold gaze"**[18] :one part sees clearly, the other perceives deeply. The inner perception must be sharp, even if your outward focus is soft.

You need to see far-off threats as though they're close, and nearby dangers with the clarity of distance. Don't get distracted by the flashiness of an opponent's movements; focus on the core—his sword, his intent.

This gaze applies to both solo and large-scale combat. You must learn to look to both sides without moving your eyes directly. It's not a skill you'll gain instantly. Practice it daily and keep it steady, no matter the situation.

Holding the Long Sword

Hold the long sword with a light grip in your thumb and index finger, your middle finger neutral—not tight, not loose—and your last two fingers firm. Avoid letting your hands feel loose or uncertain.

When you pick up your sword, your only intent should be to strike your opponent. That intention must remain constant—even as you block, deflect, or counter his sword, you may adjust

---

[18] **"Twofold gaze"** - A martial arts principle: see the whole scene (broad vision) and your opponent's intent (deep perception) at the same time.

your grip slightly in the front fingers, but never loosen your hold or allow hesitation.

Whether you're fighting or testing the blade, your grip should remain the same. There's no special "cutting grip." In general, I avoid rigidity in both hand and sword. A stiff grip is lifeless. A flexible grip brings power. Remember that.

Footwork

Step with your heels grounded and your toes slightly lifted. Whether you're moving quickly or slowly, with big steps or small, your feet should move as they would during normal walking. I do not recommend footwork that's jumpy, unsteady, or fixed in place.

There's an important concept called **"Yin-Yang footwork."**[19] This means not always leading with the same foot. Instead, let your feet move left-right, right-left—whether you're attacking, retreating, or parrying. Avoid favoring one side.

The Five Positions

There are five primary stances: High, Middle, Low, Right, and Left. Every variation of posture falls into one of these five.

---

[19] **"Yin-Yang footwork"** - Symbolic of balanced, alternating steps—left-right, right-left—to avoid predictable patterns.

No matter the stance, your goal should always be the same: cut the opponent. Don't focus on forming a particular posture— focus only on the strike.

Your stance should adjust depending on the situation. The High, Middle, and Low stances are decisive and stable. The Right and Left stances are adaptable and best used when obstacles are around or overhead. Choose them based on your environment.

To truly understand stances, you must first grasp the Middle stance. It is the foundation, the center of the system. In larger strategy, the Middle stance is like the commander—leading the others. The rest of the positions follow this lead. Learn to understand this clearly.

The Way of the Long Sword

Mastery of the long sword means you can wield it easily—even with just two fingers—because you've studied it deeply. Once you truly know the sword, using it becomes natural.

If you try to swing the long sword with speed alone, you'll stray from the Way. The sword must be used with calm control. If you handle it like a folding fan or a short blade, you'll fall into a habit of short, ineffective strikes. That approach won't cut through your opponent.

When you strike downward, lift the sword straight back up. If you slash sideways, return it along the same path. Always recover your sword in a logical, fluid motion. Keep your elbows wide and the movement strong. This is how to properly wield the long sword.

If you train consistently and apply the five principles of this strategy, you will develop true skill. Practice daily and refine your technique.

The Five Methods of Engagement

Center Stance Approach

The first method is known as the Center Stance. You face your opponent directly, aiming your blade toward their face. When they attack, redirect their sword to your right side and move in close along its path. Alternatively, when they strike, deflect the tip of their blade downward and hold your position. As they come in for a second attempt, use your long sword to cut their arms from underneath. This is the foundation of the first approach.

These five methods are techniques you must master by training continuously with a long sword. Once you fully understand my school's approach to long sword combat, you'll be able to counter any attack. There are no other stances beyond the five presented in my Niten Ichi-ryū style.

Upper Stance Approach

The second method starts from a high position. As your opponent attacks, strike them at the same moment. If they avoid your cut, keep your blade where it is and cut upwards from below when they attack again. You can also repeat the strike if needed.

This technique involves variations in timing and intent, which you'll grasp through consistent training in the Ichi school. Mastering all five methods of the long sword will give you victory. Practice is essential.

Lower Stance Approach

In the third method, take a low guard as if preparing to strike upwards. When the enemy charges, hit their hands from below. If they try to knock your blade down in response, strike across their upper arms horizontally with a crossing motion. This technique focuses on timing—intercepting the opponent's strike at the exact moment of their attack.

This method will come up frequently, whether you're new to strategy or already experienced. You must get used to using the long sword in this way through repeated practice.

Left Side Approach

For the fourth approach, begin with the sword held to your left side. As the enemy comes forward, hit their hands from below. If they attempt to knock down your blade while you do this, maintain the intention of striking their hands, redirect their blade's path, and cut downward from over your shoulder.

This is another essential method of the long sword, where you succeed by controlling the direction of the enemy's attack. Study this technique carefully.

Right Side Approach

The fifth method uses the Right Side stance. Respond to your opponent's attack by sweeping your sword upward across your body into an overhead position. Then deliver a straight, downward   cut.
This is a key technique for mastering the long sword. When you can use it fluently, you'll be able to handle even a heavy blade with ease. While I cannot explain every detail of how to use these five methods here, it's critical that you internalize the feeling of harmony with the long sword. You must understand large-scale timing, read your opponent's movements, and familiarize yourself with the five methods early on. These strategies—combined with proper timing and insight into the enemy's intent—will always lead to success. Take time to deeply reflect on them.

The Concept of "No-Stance"

The principle of "No-Stance" means that you don't need to be fixed in a specific sword posture. Still, there are five primary ways to hold the long sword. Whichever stance you take, it should suit the situation, the terrain, and the position of your opponent, making it easier to cut effectively.

You might move from a high stance to a middle stance as your intent lowers, or raise your sword slightly from the middle stance to adopt a high position. Similarly, you can shift from a low stance upward to the middle when needed. You can also bring the sword in from either side to transition into middle or lower positions depending on the moment.

This shifting principle is known as **"Existing Stance—Non-Existing Stance."**[20] The most important thing when you take up a sword is the determination to cut the enemy, however necessary. Every time you deflect, strike, or make contact with the opponent's blade, your intention must always be to cut them in the same movement. That mindset is essential. If you're focused only on making contact or blocking, you'll fail to cut effectively. More than anything, the goal is to complete your motion by

---

[20] **"Existing Stance—Non-Existing Stance"** - A concept meaning that while stances exist, the true strategist isn't fixed to any one—he moves freely as needed.

cutting the enemy. This must be thoroughly explored and practiced.

In large-scale strategy, these positions are known as "battle formations." These too must be aimed at winning. But rigid formations are flawed. Study this well.

Striking with Unified Timing

The **"Single Timing"**[21] concept means striking as soon as you close the distance with the enemy—before they can decide to retreat, defend, or strike. Do not hesitate, settle your spirit, or adjust your body. Hit directly and decisively in the opening moment of their indecision.

This type of timing must be trained until it becomes instinctive.

The "Two-Tiered Timing" of the Abdomen

When you attack and your opponent quickly steps back, observe their tension. Feint a strike, and when they start to relax, follow through and hit them. This is the "Abdomen Timing of Two."

This concept is hard to fully understand just by reading—it requires live instruction and personal experience. But once you've

---

[21] **"Single Timing"** - Striking instantly when you see an opening—decisively, before the enemy can react.

been shown the idea, it's not difficult to grasp.

No Form, No Plan

This method involves striking when you've chosen to attack. Move your body with force, channel your spirit, and unleash a powerful strike that comes out of nowhere, as if from emptiness. This is the "No Form, No Plan" technique.

It's one of the most critical and commonly used cuts. It requires dedication and training to understand.

The Flowing Water Cut[22]

Use this technique when you are locked in close, blade-to-blade combat. If the enemy breaks away suddenly and tries to lunge with their sword, expand your posture and presence, and deliver a slow, deliberate cut that flows from your body like still water.

This technique allows for a clean hit, but only if you train properly and can assess your opponent's skill level.

Continuous Cutting

When both you and your opponent strike at the same time and

---

[22] **"Flowing Water Cut"** - A calm, smooth strike delivered when the opponent breaks away—modeled after water's natural, unforced motion.

your swords clash, use a sweeping motion to strike multiple targets—his head, arms, and legs—in one fluid movement. This is the "Continuous Cut."

It's used frequently and must be drilled in detail to master.

The Fire and Stones Cut

This technique is for when swords meet in a heavy clash. Without raising your sword, cut with all the strength in your body, hands, and legs in one unified motion. This is the "Fire and Stones Cut"—quick and forceful. With enough training, you'll be able to strike with great power.

The Red Leaves Cut

The **Red Leaves Cut**[23] is about disarming your opponent. When they stand in a long sword stance, ready to strike or block, hit their blade forcefully using the Fire and Stones technique or something similar to "No Form, No Plan." With a sticky, controlling motion, knock down the tip of their sword. Done right, they'll drop it entirely.

Mastery comes from repeated practice.

---

[23] **"Red Leaves Cut"** - A poetic name for a disarming strike, making the enemy's sword "fall" like autumn leaves.

Using the Body Instead of the Sword

Also called "using the sword in place of the body." Normally, body and sword move together. But sometimes you can charge with your body first and strike afterward. If the enemy is unmovable, reverse the order and cut first. Usually, though, you lead with the body and follow with the blade.

You must study and practice this dynamic thoroughly.

The Difference Between Cutting and Slashing

Cutting and slashing are not the same. A cut is decisive—it carries a strong and focused intent. A slash is more like grazing or making contact, even if it's forceful enough to kill. What defines a cut is the spirit behind it.

If you first slash at an enemy's hands or legs, you must follow it up with a powerful, committed cut. A slash is merely an action; a cut is a resolution. Once you understand this, the two become indistinguishable in motion but remain different in spirit.

Train this deeply.

The Chinese Monkey Approach

The "Chinese Monkey" mindset is about keeping your arms close to your body—never extending them outward. The idea is to move in quickly and fully, with your whole body, before your opponent has a chance to strike. If you focus on not reaching out with your arms, it forces you to use your body to close the distance. Once you're within reach, it's easier to move in completely. Study this concept thoroughly.

The Sticky Body Like Lacquer

The principle of the "Lacquered Glue Body" is to stay close—completely glued—to your opponent. When you approach, make sure your head, torso, and legs all press in together. Many people move their head and legs first while their body trails behind, creating space. Instead, you must stay so tightly connected to your opponent that no gap remains between your body and his. Reflect deeply on this.

Reaching for Higher Ground

"Reaching for height" means that when you close in on your opponent, you should aim to be in a higher position than them, confidently and without hesitation. Straighten your legs, lift your hips, extend your neck—stand firm face-to-face. When you believe you've gained the higher position, attack with full force. You need to train diligently in this method.

The Art of Stickiness

When the enemy strikes and you respond with your long sword, your movement should feel adhesive. Press your blade against his, not with brute force, but with a firm, sticky resistance that keeps the swords from easily parting. Approach calmly, sticking to his weapon. Stickiness is different from entanglement: stickiness is controlled and strong, while entanglement is loose and weak. Understand this well.

Using Your Body to Strike

A body strike means entering through an opening in your opponent's guard and hitting them with your body. Turn your face slightly aside and drive your left shoulder into the opponent's chest. Come in hard, as if you're trying to bounce him away, timing your movement with your breath. With this method, it's possible to send an opponent flying ten or twenty feet—or even strike with lethal force. Train this method thoroughly.

Three Ways to Parry

There are three main ways to deflect an enemy's blow:

When he strikes, drive his sword to your right as though aiming a thrust at his eyes.

Parry by pushing his sword toward his right eye, almost like you're slicing at his neck.

If your long sword is on the shorter side, don't focus on deflecting. Instead, rush in and aim a thrust at his face using your left hand.
Keep in mind: you can always clench your left fist and punch toward the opponent's face. This must be trained regularly.

Aiming for the Face

Stabbing at the face means you commit to targeting the opponent's face by aligning your blade with his. Focus on driving the point of your sword straight along the line of contact. When you're determined to aim for the face, your opponent's posture will shift—his face and body become easier to dominate. This opens up many opportunities for victory. Always keep this technique in mind and refine it through training.

Aiming for the Heart

To stab at the heart is to attack when you can't strike cleanly due to barriers above or to the side. In those situations, thrust your blade directly into the opponent's chest, keeping your sword steady and showing him the flat of the blade to help deflect his own weapon. This technique is especially useful when fatigue sets in or your sword is no longer cutting effectively. Make sure you grasp when and how to use it.

The "Tut-TUT!" Reprimand

"Scolding" is a counterattack that comes when your opponent tries to strike back during your attack. You intercept his move with a cut from below, almost like a rising thrust meant to suppress him. The timing must be fast—cut while sharply exhaling "Tut!" then strike again, loudly: "TUT!" You'll encounter this situation often during exchanges. The key is to time your counter precisely as you raise your sword. Rehearse this rhythm constantly.

The Slapping Parry

The "smacking parry" is used when your sword collides with the opponent's. Rather than blocking with strength, meet his blow in rhythm—smack his sword and immediately follow through with a cut. The goal isn't to overpower but to use the rhythm of the clash to your advantage. If your timing is good, no matter how hard the blades connect, your own sword won't be pushed back. Practice until this becomes second nature.

Facing Multiple Opponents

"When facing many enemies," draw both your long sword and your companion sword and adopt a wide stance, arms spread.

The strategy is to move side to side, responding to attackers as they come from every direction. Focus on whoever attacks first. Keep your vision wide and alert, switching sides and striking alternately with both swords. Do not stand idle—cut down the attackers as they approach, pushing back from the side they came. Herd the enemies together as though stringing up fish, and when they're grouped, strike with overwhelming force to keep them from spreading out.

Gaining the Upper Hand in Combat

Understanding how to win with the long sword is not something that can be fully captured in words. Only through consistent training can you develop the instincts to succeed.

Oral tradition: *"The true Way of strategy is found in the long sword."*

One Decisive Cut

Victory can be won with a single, deliberate strike—the spirit of "one cut." This level of mastery is only possible if you deeply understand the way of strategy. With enough practice, your technique will flow naturally, and you'll be able to win whenever you choose. Train constantly.

Direct Transmission

"Direct Communication"[24] refers to how the NiTo Ichi school's true method is passed down—through direct experience.

Oral tradition: *"Teach your body the strategy."*

What's written here is a summary of the Ichi school's method. To truly learn how to win with the long sword, you must first absorb the five techniques and five stances. Let the movement of the sword become natural to you. Your timing, your body, and your spirit must all be in harmony. Whether you're fighting one opponent or many, you'll then begin to grasp the value of strategy.

Study each principle one at a time. With real combat experience, their meaning will reveal itself over time. Be deliberate. Be patient. Let the virtues of this path soak into you. Raise your sword in battle with this mindset, and keep that spirit every time you engage an opponent.

Step by step, walk the long road of the warrior.

Dedicate years to mastering strategy and becoming one with the warrior's spirit. Let each day's victory be an improvement over

---

[24] **"Direct Communication"** - Musashi emphasizes that true understanding of strategy comes through hands-on instruction, not just reading.

yesterday's self. Tomorrow, defeat those less trained. And to overcome greater opponents, follow this book strictly—do not let distractions pull your heart away. Even if you defeat someone, if it's not by what you've truly learned, it's not the real Way.

If you truly achieve the Way of victory, you can defeat dozens. What remains to be developed is your skill in battle and duels— refined only through real combat.

The Second Year of Shoho, the 12th Day of the 5th Month (1645)
Teruo Magonojo – SHINMEN MUSASHI

Analysis of The Water Book

The Water Book flows with the same qualities as water itself—fluid, adaptable, and quietly powerful. Musashi uses it to teach the core techniques of the long sword, not just physically, but mentally and strategically. He reminds us that the warrior's mindset should be the same in daily life as in battle: calm, focused, alert, and unshaken.

This book is deeply practical. Musashi teaches how to hold the sword, how to move, how to see, and how to respond to the enemy's energy. He introduces five fighting stances and five methods of engagement, but warns that no stance is fixed—strategy must stay flexible, like water adjusting to its container.

Beyond form, Musashi stresses spirit and timing. Striking isn't about speed or strength, but about cutting with intent and presence. The long sword becomes an extension of your mind. Through daily training, posture becomes natural, reaction becomes instinct, and victory becomes effortless.

Ultimately, this chapter blends swordsmanship with wisdom. It's not about tricks—it's about being fully present, fully prepared, and fully aligned in body, mind, and spirit.

Key Lessons from The Water Book

1. **Train until technique becomes instinct** — the body must move with natural skill, not forced effort.

2. **Posture and spirit are one** — how you stand in life is how you fight in battle.

3. **Timing beats speed** — a well-timed cut wins over a fast one.

4. **See with a "twofold gaze"** — take in both the big picture and subtle intent.

5. **Use strategy like water** — flow with conditions, adapt your form, and never stay rigid.

6. **Victory comes from precision and presence**, not just power.

In short

The Water Book teaches that **mastery isn't about moves—it's about mindset**. Musashi blends the physical and the mental, showing that the true strategist flows with awareness, calm, and sharp control. Learn the sword, but also learn to see, move, and think like water. That's the real Way.

The Fire Book

In this chapter, called *The Fire Book*, I compare combat to fire—fierce, fast, and decisive.

Most people misunderstand what strategy really is. They focus too much on small details—like using only the fingers instead of the whole hand. It's like judging a duel by the length of someone's forearm or the flick of a fan. They obsess over small tricks—like how to move the hands or feet with a wooden training sword—without grasping the bigger picture.

In my approach to strategy, training to defeat your opponent means constantly engaging in real combat scenarios. You learn how to live, how to face death, and how to understand the essence of swordsmanship. You learn to judge the force of an attack and grasp the deeper mechanics of the sword—its edge and its back.

Minor techniques won't save you in real combat, especially when fighting in full armor. My method is built for survival—even if you're up against five or ten enemies. There's a principle that says, "If one warrior can defeat ten enemies, then a thousand warriors can overcome ten thousand." That's something worth exploring.

Of course, it's not practical to gather thousands of fighters for daily training. But one person, through solo practice, can master strategy deeply—learning how to analyze the enemy's methods, judge their strength, and understand how to apply strategy on a large scale. That's how you prepare to defeat ten thousand opponents.

Anyone who wants to truly understand my method must train relentlessly, morning and night. With steady effort, you refine your skill, let go of ego, and develop extraordinary talent. Over time, you'll gain abilities that seem almost supernatural. That's the true power of strategy.

Reading the Environment

Always be aware of your surroundings.

Position yourself with the sun behind you so it blinds the enemy. If that's not possible, try to keep the sun on your right. Indoors, position yourself with the entrance behind you or to your right. Make sure your back is protected, your left side is open, and your right hand is free to draw your sword.

At night, if you can see your opponent, stand with a fire behind you and the entrance to your right. Apply the same positioning principles as you would during the day. Take higher ground when possible. For example, in a traditional home, the *kamiza* (the

place of honor)[25] is seen as the elevated spot—symbolically and tactically.

During a fight, try to drive the enemy toward your left. Push them into difficult or awkward areas—places where movement is restricted. Once your opponent is in a tight spot, don't give them the chance to regroup. Keep pressing. Indoors, drive them toward doorways, beams, pillars—any structural obstacle. Don't let them gain awareness of their position.

Always try to push your opponent toward bad footing or corner them near obstructions. Use the terrain to gain the upper hand. You must study and train this thoroughly.

The Three Methods for Taking Initiative

There are three primary ways to gain the upper hand:

- **Ken No Sen** – Strike first to take control.

- **Tai No Sen** – Let the enemy strike first, then seize the initiative.

- **Tai Tai No Sen** – Attack at the same moment as the

---

[25] **"Kamiza (the place of honor)"** - In traditional Japanese homes, the kamiza is the seat of honor—usually furthest from the entrance. Symbolically and tactically, it represents higher ground.

enemy, but with greater force and timing.[26]

These are the only true ways to take the lead. Gaining the initiative is one of the most critical aspects of strategy. It requires awareness, adaptability, and the ability to read your opponent's intent. While the details are hard to describe in words, the essence lies in knowing how to act first—or how to turn your enemy's first move into your own advantage.

1. Ken No Sen – Striking First

When you decide to make the first move, do so calmly but swiftly. Sometimes you can act like you're charging hard, but keep your spirit contained, waiting for the right moment to strike.

Alternatively, come at the enemy with overwhelming energy. As you get close, quicken your steps slightly to throw them off balance and strike decisively.

You can also move forward with a calm mindset and a constant intention to overpower them completely—from start to finish. The goal is to dominate them internally, even before the sword makes contact.

---

[26] **"Ken No Sen / Tai No Sen / Tai Tai No Sen"** - These are classic timing strategies in Japanese swordsmanship: strike first, counterattack, or attack simultaneously but more decisively.

These are all ways to apply *Ken No Sen*.

2. Tai No Sen – Seizing the Advantage After the Enemy Moves

If your opponent attacks first, stay composed and act weak or vulnerable. As soon as they get close and let their guard down, launch a sudden, strong counterattack.

Another method is to meet their attack with even greater force, breaking their rhythm and exploiting the chaos to win.

This is the principle of *Tai No Sen*.

3. Tai Tai No Sen – Simultaneous Attack

If the enemy attacks quickly, respond with equal calmness and power. Target their weakness as they close in, and strike with force.

If they attack slowly and carefully, watch them closely. Let your body move fluidly with theirs, match their timing, and then strike fast and hard.

This is *Tai Tai No Sen*.

You can't fully learn these concepts through explanation alone. You must train to truly understand them. It's not about always striking first; even if they move before you, you can still guide them into your trap. When you can anticipate and control your opponent's actions, you've already won. Train hard to reach that level.

Pinning the Pillow

"To pin the pillow" means never letting your opponent lift their head or gain momentum.

In battle, it's dangerous to be controlled by your enemy. You must be the one leading the dance. Of course, your opponent is trying to do the same—but if you keep them suppressed, they won't be able to act.

You must learn to shut down their attacks, deflect their thrusts, and break free when they try to grapple you. This is what **"pinning the pillow"**[27] is all about. When you truly understand this principle, you'll be able to anticipate everything they try to do and stop it before it happens.

Your goal is to stop their useful moves, not their useless ones. Blocking only is too defensive. True mastery is suppressing their effective strategies, ruining their plans, and then taking full

---

[27] **"Pinning the pillow"** - A metaphor for suppressing the enemy's actions before they can even begin. Control them at the source.

control of the fight. This is how you become a true strategist.

Study and train this concept carefully.

Crossing the Ford

"Crossing at a ford"[28] refers to making a decisive move when the time is right. It's like navigating a narrow channel at sea or crossing a broad expanse at just the right spot.

In life, these moments come often—times when others hesitate, but you choose to move forward. When the route is clear, the conditions are favorable, and the opportunity presents itself, you must act. If the wind changes before you reach your destination, then row hard to complete the journey.

This mindset also applies to strategy. Learn to read your enemy, understand your own strengths, and act when you can gain the upper hand. Like a skilled captain who chooses the perfect crossing point, you must learn to move at the right moment to attack your opponent's weak spot and claim victory.

Whether in a small duel or a large-scale battle, this mindset is essential. Study it well.

---

[28] **"Crossing at a ford"** - A metaphor for seizing an opportunity at the right time, like crossing a river where it's shallow and safe.

Understanding Timing

"To know the times" means understanding the rhythm of the battle. Is the enemy's morale rising or falling? What is their mental state? By observing their energy and choosing the right positioning, you can adjust your actions to take advantage.

In one-on-one combat, you must act at the moment your opponent's style and intent become clear. Analyze their background, strengths, and weaknesses. Attack in a way they don't expect, matching your timing to their rhythm and disrupting it.

If your skill is high enough, you'll gain insight into what your opponent is thinking. With deep knowledge of strategy, you can see through their plans and find countless chances to win.

This is something you must study with dedication.

Overpowering the Attack

The idea of **"overpowering the sword"**[29] is a key principle in strategy. On a battlefield, when the enemy starts by firing arrows or guns and then charges, we can't respond effectively if we're still reloading our weapons or preparing to shoot. The right mindset is

---

[29] **"Overpowering the sword"** - Refers to dominating the opponent's attack forcefully and decisively—physically, mentally, and spiritually.

to strike swiftly while they're still firing. The goal is to win by overwhelming them even as they attack.

In one-on-one combat, you won't win by casually swinging your sword after the enemy strikes. You need to stop them right as they begin their attack—with the intention of crushing their momentum completely, leaving them no chance to come back.

"Overpowering" isn't just about physical force. It involves using your whole body, your mindset, and your sword. You have to commit fully so the enemy can't launch a second attack. This is the essence of acting first and decisively. Once you begin your move, don't just aim to land a blow—follow through relentlessly. Learn this thoroughly.

Understanding Collapse

Everything can fall apart—buildings, people, even your opponent—especially when their rhythm is thrown off.

In large-scale warfare, if the enemy starts to crumble, you must push forward and take advantage of it immediately. If you hesitate, they might recover and counterattack.

In individual combat, there are times when your opponent loses timing or composure. If you don't act, they'll quickly regain control and won't make the same mistake again. Watch closely for these moments of collapse, pursue relentlessly, and make sure they can't bounce back. Strike with full force and finish the fight. You need to understand exactly how to do this.

Stepping Into the Enemy's Mind

"Becoming the enemy" means putting yourself in their position—thinking exactly how they think. For example, people often imagine a cornered thief as someone dangerous and hard to defeat. But if you see things from his point of view, you realize he's trapped and desperate. He becomes prey. You become the hunter.

In large-scale strategy, it's common to assume the enemy is stronger than they really are, making you overly cautious. But if your troops are well-trained, and you understand strategic principles and know how to beat the enemy, there's no need for fear.

The same goes for single combat. If you look at your opponent and think, "He's a true master who knows all the strategies," you've already lost. Don't do that. Always think from his perspective.

Breaking the Stalemate

"Releasing four hands"[30] refers to a situation where you and the enemy are equally matched in spirit, and nothing seems to break the tie. In these moments, you must let go of that locked mindset and win by using an unexpected tactic.

In large-scale battles, if you find yourself in a deadlock, don't give up—that's just part of life. Let go of the tension, switch your approach, and use a strategy your opponent won't see coming.

In one-on-one combat, if you're stuck in a similar stalemate, break it by changing your mindset. Use a technique that fits the situation and throws the opponent off. You must be able to recognize and act on this when the time comes.

Revealing the Hidden Intent

"Moving the shade"[31] applies when you can't read your opponent's intentions.

In a larger battle, if the enemy's position is unclear, make a strong move as if you're about to attack. This will force them to reveal

---

[30] **"Releasing four hands"** - A poetic expression for breaking a stalemate or deadlock in combat by changing rhythm or tactic unexpectedly.

[31] **"Moving the shade"** - Forcing the opponent to reveal their hidden intentions, often through feints or probing attacks.

their strategy. Once you understand their setup, you can beat them with a more effective method.

In personal combat, if the opponent takes a stance that hides their plan, you can fake a move. Thinking they've seen your strategy, they'll react and expose their intentions. Once they do, take advantage of the opening and win decisively. But if you're careless, you'll miss your moment. Study this carefully.

Pinning Down the Intent

"Holding down a shadow" is used when you can sense the enemy's intent to attack.

In larger strategy, if the enemy is about to make a move, act like you're completely shutting it down. This can force them to second-guess themselves. Then, change your approach and strike with the energy of emptiness—what Musashi calls the "Void" spirit.

In one-on-one fights, when you sense the opponent's intention, suppress it with perfect timing and strike first before they act. This is a crucial concept you must learn deeply.

Passing on the Spirit

There's a concept where feelings or states can be "passed on"—

like sleepiness, yawning, or even time.

In large-scale battles, if the enemy is nervous or in a hurry, stay calm and unfazed. Display a sense of total ease. This calmness will influence the enemy and they'll begin to relax. Once you see that shift, strike with a sudden and strong attack powered by the energy of emptiness.

In single combat, the same applies. Relax your mind and body. Then, when your opponent relaxes too, unleash a fast and powerful attack. This idea of "getting someone drunk" is similar—it's about influencing their state of mind. You can infect them with a sense of boredom, carelessness, or weakness. Study this thoroughly.

Causing a Loss of Balance

Many things can throw a person off balance—danger, fatigue, or sudden shock. You need to explore and understand this fully.

In large-scale warfare, disrupting your opponent's balance is essential. Strike where they least expect it, catch them off guard, and then press your advantage before they recover.

In one-on-one combat, act slow and easy at first. Then suddenly explode into action. Don't give your opponent any time to breathe or regroup. Learn to sense the right moment to strike and win. Get used to how this feels.

Instilling Fear

Fear often arises from the unexpected. In large-scale combat, you don't always need a visual display to scare the enemy. Loud noises, making a small force seem large, or launching sudden attacks from the side can cause panic. These tactics disrupt the enemy's rhythm, and mastering how to exploit that fear can lead you to victory.

In one-on-one combat, you can do the same—catch your opponent off guard and shake him using your stance, your sword, or your voice. Train yourself to understand this well.

Blending With the Opponent

When you're locked in a struggle and can't push forward, the best move might be to stop resisting and merge with your opponent— become one with them. From that connection, you can apply the right technique at the right moment to win.

This strategy works in both large battles and individual fights. Often, victory comes from staying close and entangled rather than pulling away. Study this thoroughly.

Attacking the Weak Points

Strong structures can't be moved by brute force, so you should aim for the corners. In large-scale battles, hitting the edges of the enemy formation can cause the entire force to lose its spirit. Once the outer positions fall, follow up immediately to finish the enemy off.

In solo combat, the same principle applies. Wounding the "corners" of your opponent's body weakens them and opens the path to victory. Master this skill.

Creating Confusion

This tactic is all about breaking your opponent's focus. In warfare, use your troops to disturb the enemy's mental clarity. If they start thinking, "Where are they attacking? Here? There? Fast? Slow?"—you've already taken control of the fight.

In personal duels, confuse your opponent with unpredictable moves. Fake a strike or approach, then attack when they're unsure. Confusion disrupts their rhythm, and in that moment, you win. This principle is essential—learn it deeply.

The Three Battle Cries[32]

There are three types of battle cries: one before the fight, one during, and one after. Your voice expresses energy and intent. We shout at storms, fires, and during moments of intensity—it's a natural part of life.

In full-scale combat, begin with a loud shout to signal the start of battle. During the clash, let your voice drop low and powerful as you strike. After victory, shout again in triumph. These are the three cries.

In single combat, shout "Ei!" as you move to strike—this startles the enemy. Follow that up with your attack, then shout once more after the enemy is defeated, to declare victory. This is known as the "before and after" voice. Don't shout while swinging your sword for show. Instead, use the shout to sync with your rhythm. Train in this skill seriously.

Mixing It Up

When facing an enemy force, strike one of their strongholds. If they fall back, quickly shift to strike another stronghold nearby. This tactic is like navigating a winding mountain trail—constantly

---

[32] **"Three Battle Cries"** - In samurai combat, these vocal shouts mark the beginning, middle, and end of battle—used to energize and intimidate.

changing direction while keeping momentum.

This same principle applies even when you're fighting many alone. Hit one group hard, then immediately move to the next. The key is understanding their rhythm, then striking without hesitation. In one-on-one combat, apply this idea to the opponent's strong points—advance without retreating. This spirit of constant forward motion is what "mingling" truly means. Learn it fully.

Crushing the Enemy

To crush your opponent is to regard them as already defeated. In large-scale battles, if your enemies are few or their morale is weak and disorganized, strike them like pulling a hat down over their eyes—swift and total. If you go too easy, they may recover. Learn how to crush decisively, like gripping with full force.

In single combat, if the opponent is less skilled, off-rhythm, or retreating, don't hesitate. Overwhelm him completely without giving him a chance to catch his breath or recover. The goal is to end it before he regains his footing. Study this with intensity.

The Mountain-Sea Principle

This concept teaches that repeating the same move over and over is a mistake. Doing something twice might be necessary—but rarely should you try it a third time. If an attack fails once, it's unlikely to work again. If you try the same move twice and still fail, change your approach entirely.

If the enemy prepares for the mountains, strike like the sea. If he prepares for the sea, strike like the mountains. Constant change and adaptation are vital. Train in this deeply.

Striking the Core

Sometimes you may seem to have the upper hand, but if your enemy's spirit remains unbroken, the fight isn't over. Winning on the surface means little if your opponent's will is still intact. That's why you must learn how to destroy the enemy's spirit at its core.

This involves penetrating with your sword, your body, and your spirit. It's not something that can be summarized easily—it must be lived and experienced. Once the enemy's spirit is truly broken, your own spirit can rest. But if he remains strong inside, it's difficult to fully defeat him. Train this principle for both battlefield tactics and personal duels.

Starting Fresh

There are times when the clash between you and your enemy becomes stuck, with no clear way forward. When that happens, you must drop your current approach, reset your mindset, and find a new rhythm. This shift in spirit is how you find the path to victory.

This idea also applies in large-scale battles. When the flow of combat becomes tangled, think fresh, move fresh, and win through a different method. Study this carefully.

Rat's Head, Ox's Neck

The phrase **"rat's head, ox's neck"**[33] reflects a mindset vital in combat. When you and your opponent are both fixated on minor details and caught in a tangled state of mind, it's essential to remember that the true path of strategy must be both agile and strong—like a rat's nimble head and an ox's sturdy neck.

If you find yourself stuck in small matters, shift your mindset instantly to one that's broad and expansive. You must learn to alternate between narrow focus and wide perspective as needed.

This way of thinking is central to mastering strategy. A warrior must carry this mindset not only in combat but also in daily life. Whether you're engaged in a large-scale campaign or a one-on-one duel, never lose sight of this balance in spirit.

---

[33] **"Rat's head, ox's neck"** - A metaphor about combining agility (rat) with strength and endurance (ox)—representing flexible yet grounded strategy.

The Commander Understands His Soldiers

In my approach to strategy, this idea applies universally: "The commander understands his soldiers."

Think of your enemy as if they were your own troops. With that mindset, you can predict and manipulate their movements. You can lead them as if you were their general, turning their actions to your advantage.

This is a skill you must truly understand and internalize.

Letting Go of the Sword

There are many subtle states of mind involved in the act of letting go of the sword.

There is a mindset where you achieve victory without even drawing your weapon. And there is also the situation where, even while holding your sword, you fail to win.

These nuances can't be fully explained with words—they must be experienced and understood through diligent practice.

Becoming Like a Rock

Once you've truly absorbed the Way of strategy, you can make your body immovable, like solid rock. When you reach this state, nothing can touch or shake you—no matter how many forces surround you.

This is what it means to have the **"body of a rock."**[34]

It's something passed down by word of mouth.

Everything above captures the thoughts that have stayed with me throughout my years of practicing the Ichi school of swordsmanship. I've written it down as it came to me, so the flow may seem somewhat disorganized. Expressing it clearly in writing is no easy task.

This book is a spiritual guide for anyone determined to follow the Way.

From a young age, I've been devoted to the path of strategy. I've trained my hands, hardened my body, and pursued the many mental disciplines required in swordsmanship.

When I observe practitioners from other schools who fixate on theory and hand technique, I notice that—despite their outward skill—they often lack true spirit.

Many believe they are cultivating both mind and body, but in fact,

---

[34] **"Body of a rock"** - An ideal state of immovability—total composure and physical/spiritual stability, central to Musashi's strategic philosophy.

this kind of practice obstructs the real path. The negative effects linger and distort their growth. Because of this, the authentic Way of strategy is fading and close to vanishing.

The real essence of swordsmanship is not in forms or theory—it lies in defeating your opponent in battle. Nothing else.

If you dedicate yourself to understanding and living by the wisdom of this strategy, you will never need to doubt your ability to win.

Written on the twelfth day of the fifth month, in the second year of Shohō (1645)

Teruo Magonojo – SHINMEN MUSASHI

Analysis of The Fire Book

The Fire Book is Musashi's guide to real combat—fast, fierce, and decisive, just like fire. He warns against focusing too much on technique or appearance. Strategy isn't about small tricks; it's about understanding timing, intent, and how to win—not just strike.

This chapter shifts the focus from inner posture (like in the Water Book) to aggression, initiative, and domination. Musashi explains that in battle, whether against one or many, you must train your mind and body to act without hesitation. Strategy is about pressing the advantage, exploiting fear, imbalance, terrain, and reading your enemy's rhythm.

Key ideas like Ken No Sen, Tai No Sen, and Tai Tai No Sen teach you how to control initiative—whether you strike first, counter, or clash simultaneously with greater force. Musashi also explores deeper strategic principles like crossing the ford (acting at the right time), pinning the pillow (controlling the opponent), and becoming like a rock (achieving spiritual immovability).

Above all, this book reminds us that strategy is for winning, not for showing skill. If your sword doesn't defeat your opponent, your form means nothing.

Key Lessons from The Fire Book

1. **Initiative is everything** — learn when to strike first, when to wait, and when to break the rhythm.

2. **Real combat reveals truth** — flashy techniques fail in the chaos of battle.

3. **Control your opponent's rhythm** — dominate their intent before they act.

4. **Adapt your spirit** — be flexible like water, but burn with focused purpose like fire.

5. **Strike where they're weak** — target imbalance, hesitation, or overconfidence.

6. **Victory comes from presence and precision**, not brute strength or form.

In short

The Fire Book teaches how to win—not just with the sword, but with your entire presence. It's a manual for mastering pressure, seizing opportunity, and acting decisively. In Musashi's words: don't polish your technique for show—train to survive, dominate, and prevail.

The Wind Book

In mastering strategy, it's essential to understand how other schools operate. That's why in this section, I've described the methods of various other traditions. Without comparing them to my own Ichi school, it would be difficult to fully grasp the essence of my teachings.

Some schools focus on brute strength, favoring oversized swords. Others are built around the short sword—known as the **kodachi**[35]. Some place great emphasis on mastering countless sword techniques, treating the physical movements as the "appearance" and the deeper meaning as the "core." But none of these, I argue, truly represent the real Way of strategy.

In this book, I've laid out clearly what is right and wrong in those schools, what's useful and what's not. My Ichi school takes a different approach. Many other schools treat their accomplishments like products—decorating them, dressing them up, and selling them for recognition or money. That's not true strategy.

There are even so-called strategists who focus solely on

---

[35] **"Kodachi"** - A short sword, smaller than a katana, used primarily in close quarters. Some schools based their style on it, but Musashi critiques relying too heavily on short or long weapons alone.

swordsmanship—spinning the long sword with flair or putting all their effort into body form and posture. But is showmanship alone enough to win in battle? I don't believe so. This misses the heart of strategy.

In this chapter, I highlight the weaknesses I've observed in other schools. You need to study these closely to understand the real value of my Ni To Ichi style.

Schools That Favor Extra-Long Swords

Some schools are fond of using especially long swords. From my perspective, this reflects a lack of depth in their understanding of strategy. Their approach relies on staying far from the opponent and hoping the length of their sword gives them an edge. But this mindset misses the fundamental idea of cutting your opponent however necessary.

There's a saying: **"An extra inch gives you the upper hand."**[36] But this kind of thinking shows a lack of strategic insight. Leaning too much on the length of your blade, without truly understanding how to fight, reveals a weak spirit. Maybe there's some doctrinal reason behind their preference, but even then, it

---

[36] **"An extra inch gives you the upper hand"** - A traditional proverb that assumes reach equals advantage. Musashi disagrees, emphasizing mindset and adaptability over physical reach.

doesn't hold up in real combat.

Can't someone fight and win with a short sword, even without a longer one? When you're in close range, a long sword can become a burden. It takes more space to swing and slows you down, putting you at a disadvantage compared to someone using a shorter weapon.

There's an old saying: "Large and small go hand in hand." So I'm not saying long swords are inherently bad. What I reject is the obsession with them. In broader military terms, we can compare large armies to long swords and small forces to short ones. Fewer soldiers can still defeat larger numbers—history proves it.

If you're caught in a tight space and can't stop thinking about using your long sword, or if you're in a building with only your sidearm, you're not thinking strategically. Not everyone has the same physical strength either. My teachings warn against narrow, rigid thinking. Reflect on this carefully.

The "Strong Sword" Mindset

You shouldn't think of your long sword in terms of strength or weakness. If your only goal is to strike with force, your technique will become crude, and you'll struggle to win. Focusing on hitting hard leads to overexertion and ineffective attacks—even in sword testing, trying to cut too forcefully is counterproductive.

When you're in a fight, don't think about hitting hard—or softly. Just focus on cutting and eliminating your opponent. Nothing else matters. If you aim to overpower the opponent's sword with raw strength, you'll likely end up off-balance, your own weapon pushed away as a result. That's why the phrase "the strongest wins" doesn't really hold up in true strategy.

In large-scale combat, relying on strength alone leads to grueling battles when both sides are evenly matched. Victory in that scenario comes down to more than brute force. It depends on proper principles and strategy.

In my school, we win through insight and understanding—not through flash or force. Learn this deeply.

The Use of Shorter Long Swords

Some schools prefer slightly shorter long swords, believing they allow quicker movements in close combat. Historically, *tachi* and *katana* represented long and short swords. Strong warriors could wield even the longest swords with ease, so why lean toward shorter blades?

Some fighters try to time their attacks for when the enemy's guard is down—waiting for a flourish or an opening. But that kind of reactive strategy doesn't hold up in chaotic, close-range combat or when facing multiple opponents.

Trying to dart in and out with a short sword may seem agile, but when overwhelmed, you're forced to parry constantly and lose control. This approach strays from true strategy.

A better method is to confuse and overwhelm your enemy with confident, direct movements—hold your stance firmly and make your opponent dodge and retreat. That's how you maintain control. In broader warfare, the same principle applies: overwhelm your enemy quickly and decisively.

Unfortunately, many people become fixated on dodging, retreating, and reacting. They get stuck in this mindset, which makes them easy for the enemy to manipulate. True strategy is direct and commanding. You must take control and force your opponent to respond to you.

Schools That Emphasize Too Many Techniques

Some schools boast dozens of sword methods to impress beginners. But this is just marketing—they're selling strategy like a product. That's not the right spirit.

Here's the truth: taking a life, whether in war or self-defense, isn't something that needs countless techniques. Killing is killing—whether done by a trained warrior or someone completely unskilled. There may be slight variations—thrusting, slashing—but the principle remains the same.

You don't need fancy refinements. Still, depending on the environment, your sword may be restricted—walls, ceilings, narrow paths—so it's wise to understand the **five main directions of attack**[37] and how to position your sword accordingly.

Anything beyond those five—twisting, bending your body, jumping around—isn't true strategy. My method is simple: I keep my posture and intent firm and straight, and I let the enemy be the one who contorts and overreaches.

Victory comes when your opponent loses composure. That's when you strike. You must understand this well.

The Idea of "Attitude" in Sword Schools

Some schools place a lot of emphasis on sword stances or "attitudes." But this way of thinking is misguided. These stances are only relevant when there's no actual fight happening. Historically, "attitudes" were meant for times of defense—guarding castles, preparing formations—not one-on-one combat.

In a duel, your goal is always to take initiative. "Attitude" implies passivity—waiting to be attacked. That's the wrong mindset.

---

[37] **"Five main directions of attack"** - Fundamental vectors in traditional sword combat: up, down, left, right, and thrust. Musashi builds his entire system on mastering these rather than dozens of flashy techniques.

In true strategy, you must break your opponent's posture. Strike where he's lazy, throw him off rhythm, provoke and scare him. Attack when he's off-balance, and you can win.

I reject the defensive mindset of "attitude." In my teaching, I use the concept of **No Attitude**[38]—meaning there is no fixed stance. You adapt and dominate.

In large-scale warfare, at the beginning of battle, we set up our forces based on our strength, enemy numbers, and terrain. That's preparation. But once the battle begins, the mindset shifts.

There's a major difference between defending and attacking. Standing firm, parrying blows, and holding your ground is like forming a solid wall of weapons. But when you attack, you must shift gears entirely—like pulling the very spears from the wall and charging ahead.

This is something you must study and grasp deeply.

Where to Look During Combat — A Critique of Other Schools

Some martial traditions teach that you should fix your eyes on your opponent's sword. Others say to watch the hands, the face,

---

[38] **"No Attitude"** - Musashi's principle of having no fixed stance. True strategy means adapting posture to the situation, rather than relying on set forms.

the feet, and so on. But focusing your gaze on any specific body part can scatter your mind and disrupt your strategy.

Let me explain this more clearly. Professional athletes, like football players, don't just stare at the ball—they perform skillfully by reading the whole field. When you've trained extensively in something, you're no longer reliant on sight alone. A master musician may have a score in front of them or a warrior may flourish their sword freely, but this doesn't mean they are fixated on specific objects or making random movements—it means they've learned to perceive things naturally.

In martial strategy, once you've experienced many real fights, you'll be able to read the opponent's movements and intentions without needing to stare at individual actions. When you've mastered the Way, you begin to sense the enemy's spirit. In larger-scale combat, what matters most is the strength of the enemy force as a whole.

There are two ways of seeing: "sight" and "perception." Sight is about physically looking. Perception involves focusing deeply on your opponent's spirit, watching the battlefield, and sensing the shifts in momentum. That kind of awareness leads to victory.

In one-on-one duels, don't get caught up in small details. As I've already said, if you obsess over little things and lose track of the bigger picture, your mind will become foggy, and you'll lose your edge. Reflect on this and train seriously.

Footwork — A Critique of Other Schools

Many schools promote different types of foot movement: light steps, leaping steps, bouncing, pressing down, or quick darting techniques. From my perspective, these methods are flawed.

I don't like the floating step, because it often leads to instability. In the Way of the warrior, you must always stand firmly.

Jumping footwork is also not good—it builds a habit of unnecessary hopping, which leads to a jittery mindset. There's rarely a good reason to jump in combat. Springy footwork creates indecision. The pressing step is too passive, which I especially dislike.

Other styles promote fast-stepping techniques like the **"crow's foot"**[39] and similar moves. But remember, in real battle you may find yourself fighting on muddy fields, uneven ground, riverbanks, or narrow paths—places where jumping or quick footwork is impossible.

---

[39] **"Crow's foot" footwork** - A nickname for complex footwork promoted in some schools. Musashi criticizes it as impractical for real-world conditions like mud or uneven terrain.

In my method, your footwork remains steady and natural, like walking down a street. You should never lose control of your feet. Adapt your speed based on your opponent—sometimes faster, sometimes slower—but always with balance.

Good footwork matters just as much in large-scale battle. If you rush in too fast without reading the opponent's rhythm, you'll become disorganized and lose. But if you move too slowly, you might miss the moment to strike when the enemy is vulnerable. You must win by exploiting their confusion and not giving them any chance to recover. Practice this principle thoroughly.

Speed — A Critique of Other Schools

Speed, as most understand it, isn't a core part of true martial strategy. Whether something seems fast or slow depends entirely on whether it matches the proper rhythm. A true strategist doesn't need to look fast.

For example, some travelers can walk 100 or even 120 miles in a day, but they don't run all day to do it—they manage their pace efficiently. Meanwhile, an inexperienced runner might look like they've been sprinting nonstop, but they're really just moving poorly.

In dance, a skilled performer can sing while moving with grace, but a beginner trying the same thing will slow down and lose focus. Playing a slow, deep rhythm like the "Old Pine Tree" on a drum may seem easy, but beginners tend to lose control and become flustered.

Experts may handle fast rhythms, but rushing the beat is always a mistake. On the other hand, being too slow is also bad. True masters stay perfectly in time—they are precise, calm, and never look frantic. That's the standard you should aim for.

Speed, as most schools teach it, is actually harmful in the Way. In rough terrain—like marshes or rocky ground—you won't be able to move quickly or swing a long sword easily. If you try to slash with speed like you would with a fan or short blade, your attack won't even land properly. You must understand this deeply.

Even in large-scale combat, having a fast or scattered mindset will hurt you. Your spirit should be steady—like the weight of a heavy cushion pressing down. That way, you'll never be late in responding.

If your enemy rushes recklessly, respond with calm. Don't let their speed dictate your rhythm. Train thoroughly to develop this unshakable spirit.

Surface and Depth — A Critique of Other Schools

In strategy, there's no such thing as surface or depth.

In the arts, people often talk about hidden meanings, secret teachings, inner doors, and so on. But in combat, there's no such thing as attacking on the surface or cutting with "inner" technique.

When I teach, I start with straightforward techniques that are easy for students to grasp. As their understanding deepens, I introduce more subtle ideas—principles that can't be explained with words alone. True understanding comes only through experience.

In life, if you wander deep into the mountains, you might think you're getting closer to some hidden center—but instead, you just **find yourself back at the entrance**[40]. Every path has its own hidden parts, but also its own gate. In martial strategy, there's no clear line between what's hidden and what's shown.

For this reason, I don't believe in passing on my teachings through written promises or rigid codes. I gauge each student's potential and guide them directly, helping them break free from the limits of other schools and bringing them closer to the true Way.

I teach with a sincere spirit. You must dedicate yourself to this

---

[40] **"Wander deep into the mountains… find yourself back at the entrance"** - A Zen-like observation: deep knowledge often leads back to simple truths. Musashi rejects mystification in favor of direct, lived experience.

path and train with intensity.

What I've outlined above are general critiques of nine common tendencies found in other schools. I could go into detail about each specific school and their teachings—from their **"gateways" to their inner secrets**[41]—but I've deliberately chosen not to name names.

Why? Because every school interprets its ideas differently, and different people will always have different opinions. No single perspective defines the truth.

I've explained the broader patterns I see across many schools. When you look at them honestly, you'll see that people tend to fixate on either long swords or short ones, or obsess over physical strength—whether in big or small matters. That's why I don't focus on other schools' systems or secrets.

In my own style, the School of the Long Sword, there's no concept of "gate" or "interior." There are no hidden meanings in the posture of the sword. You simply stay true in spirit, and through that, realize the true Way of strategy.

Written on the twelfth day of the fifth month, Shoho Year

---

[41] **"Gateways"** and **"inner secrets"** - Refers to how many martial arts schools divided teachings into outer/public and inner/secret levels. Musashi rejects this division.

Two (1645)[42]

Teruo Magonojo – SHINMEN MUSASHI

---

[42] **"Shohō Year Two (1645)"** - This is when Musashi finished writing the text, shortly before his death in self-imposed retreat at Reigandō cave.

Analysis of The Wind Book

The Wind Book is Musashi's critical reflection on other martial traditions. "Wind" means "style" or "tradition," and here he dismantles the methods of rival schools—not out of pride, but to sharpen the contrast with his own. His message is clear: most schools are distracted by form, flair, and fixed ideas.

Musashi warns against schools that fixate on long or short swords, complicated techniques, flashy footwork, or superficial speed. He critiques their obsession with hidden meanings, rigid stances, and layered "secrets." All of it, he says, misses the essence of strategy: to win, not to impress.

Instead, his Ichi school emphasizes clarity, flexibility, and simplicity grounded in experience. No fixed stances. No secret techniques. No mysticism. Just strategy born from direct engagement with life and combat.

Key Lessons from The Wind Book

1. **Don't worship technique** — too many moves confuse the purpose of the sword.

2. **Form is secondary** — what matters is victory, not aesthetics.

3. **Be adaptable** — fixed stances and footwork fail in real combat.

4. **See beyond the surface** — strategy isn't in flash, but in perception and rhythm.

5. **No "inner secrets"** — true knowledge is gained through experience, not guarded rituals.

In short

The Wind Book is Musashi's sharp call to cut through tradition's illusions. He shows how other schools cloud the path with ego, performance, and overly complicated methods. His strategy is clear, direct, and deeply rooted in reality—not style. To follow the Way, you must let go of appearance and pursue truth.

The Book of the Void[43]

This final section explains the Ni To Ichi Way of strategy—recorded here as the "Book of the Void."

The "Void" refers to the state of absolute nothingness. It's not something that can be fully grasped through ordinary human knowledge. By understanding the things that *do* exist, we can start to perceive what *does not*. That is the essence of the void.

Many people in the world misinterpret this concept. They assume that anything they don't understand must be the void—but that's not true. **That confusion is simply ignorance**[44], not genuine insight into nothingness.

This same misunderstanding happens in the martial arts. Some warriors believe that anything beyond their comprehension in combat must belong to the realm of the void. But again, this is mistaken. That's not the true void.

To truly master the Way of strategy, a warrior must fully study other martial arts and never stray from the warrior's path. Keep

---

[43] "Void" (空, kū) is a central Zen Buddhist concept—referring not to emptiness as absence, but to a formless, limitless awareness beyond logic or perception.

[44] **"That confusion is simply ignorance"** - Musashi warns against mistaking things we don't understand for something profound. Ignorance isn't the same as insight.

your mind steady. Train with discipline, every single day and every hour. **Refine your dual nature—your spirit and your intellect**[45]. Sharpen both your inner awareness and your outward perception. When your spirit is no longer clouded or confused—when all doubts have cleared—then you will begin to understand the real void.

Until you come to truly grasp the Way—whether through spiritual practice like Buddhism or through everyday reasoning—you may believe you see things clearly and correctly. But when you step back and view life through the natural laws that govern the world, you'll notice that many beliefs and doctrines actually stray from the real Way.

Understand this clearly: stay grounded in honesty and sincerity, and **let the true spirit guide you along the Way**[46]. Carry out your strategy with clarity, precision, and openness.

Eventually, you'll begin to see things from a broader perspective. You'll recognize **the void as the Way—and the Way as the**

---

[45] **"Refine your dual nature—your spirit and your intellect"** - Musashi emphasizes the unity of instinct (spirit) and reason (intellect) as key to mastering strategy—both must be disciplined.

[46] **"Let the true spirit guide you along the Way"** - Refers to makoto no kokoro—the sincere, undistorted heart that leads a warrior with clarity, honesty, and purpose.

void.[47]

Within the void there is virtue, but no evil. Wisdom exists. Principles exist. The Way exists. But the spirit itself is rooted in nothingness.

Written on the twelfth day of the fifth month, second year of Shoho (1645)

Teruo Magonojo – SHINMEN MUSASHI

---

[47] **"The void as the Way—and the Way as the void"** - A statement of non-duality: the ultimate path (strategy, life, enlightenment) is inseparable from the void—beyond technique or thought.

Analysis of The Void Book

The Void Book is the most spiritual and abstract part of *The Book of Five Rings*. Here, Musashi moves beyond combat, posture, and technique—into the realm of pure awareness. The "Void" is not emptiness in a negative sense; it is formless clarity, the space beyond ego and confusion.

Musashi warns that many mistake ignorance for enlightenment. The true Void isn't what you don't understand—it's what remains when you've understood everything clearly and let go of it all. Strategy, like life, must be lived fully and then transcended.

Key Lessons from The Void Book

1. **The Void is clarity beyond form** — not confusion, but perfect simplicity.

2. **Daily discipline clears the mind** — true strategy arises when doubt disappears.

3. **Perception expands** — when you align with natural law, the Way reveals itself.

4. **The Way and the Void are one** — mastery is not accumulation, but release.

In short

The Void Book ends Musashi's teachings with a whisper instead of a clash. When you've truly lived the Way—through combat, practice, and insight—you'll see that the final step is letting go. **Within nothingness lies everything**.

Afterword by Timeless Lore

As you reach the final page of *The Book of Five Rings*, take a moment to reflect on Musashi's enduring legacy—not just as a warrior, but as a thinker, teacher, and strategist. His words go far beyond technique; they speak to a way of life rooted in clarity, discipline, adaptability, and the relentless pursuit of mastery.

This is not merely a book about swordsmanship or combat. It is a guide to seeing the world clearly, acting with purpose, and training the body, mind, and spirit to work in harmony. The principles Musashi shares—especially those of timing, perception, and the void—remain strikingly relevant in our modern lives, whether applied to leadership, personal growth, or the quiet battles we each face daily.

We hope this edition has helped illuminate the depth of Musashi's teachings and made them accessible without losing their strength or subtlety. If this book brought you insight or inspiration, we would be truly grateful if you left an honest review on Amazon. Your feedback not only helps us improve—it also helps others discover the timeless wisdom preserved in these pages.

Thank you for joining us on this journey into the Way of strategy.

Timeless Lore

About Us

At **Timeless Lore**, our mission is to revive the wisdom of the past for today's world. We curate and adapt classic texts in history, philosophy, and spirituality—making them readable, relevant, and resonant for modern readers, while honoring the depth and intent of the originals.

We believe timeless works still have much to teach us. Whether by refining the language or adding context through thoughtful commentary, our goal is to bridge centuries of insight and bring lasting ideas into everyday life.

We're also cultivating a growing community on TikTok and Instagram, where we share ideas, spark conversations, and make ancient wisdom part of today's dialogue.

Follow us and be part of a movement to rediscover the lessons that never go out of date.

TikTok: @timeless.lore

Instagram: @timeless.lore

Printed in Dunstable, United Kingdom

70982155R00060